MW01632579

The Power of You

Lesley Diana

To my father for always pushing me to believe in the extraordinary. To my mother for always encouraging my art. To the most loving and encouraging boyfriend. To my family and friends for their unconditional support. To *you* for taking the time to read, I am eternally grateful for you choosing to do so. I hope you this collection inspires you to fall in love with the gift of every day, appreciate your potential, and go after your heart's desires. Here are 140 reminders that you deserve to live your most beautiful rewarding life.

Love Today: Choose to eagerly fall in love with every day you were gifted on earth. Only then, will you appreciate your delicate existence.

Love Yourself: Your worth will never be defined by this world, but by your very own thoughts, actions, and words. Shower yourself in kindness and grace, and forgive yourself for all your mistakes.

Adversity: Hardships will come, but they will not sink us. These are the seasons we not only overcome but grow from. Resilience, I think, is the most beautiful human superpower.

Faith: To believe in something greater than you and me, is to understand the power of our existence. Fear has no name, in the presence of faith.

Keep Going: When you don't know what happens next, and you feel like finding the nearest exit, keep going. Believe me when I say you don't want to stay in one place for the rest of this life.

Believe in You: The chances of you being here are one in 400 trillion. Your existence is pure magnificence. Believe in the power of *you*, and start making all your wildest wishes come true.

Lesley Diana

Love Today

make it your mission
to adore everything in your life
to *find* the beauty
in having limited time
if you do it right
you won't let a day go by
without allowing your heart
to be filled with love
because we only get
to do this *once*

i started romanticizing
my life
one day
at a time

every morning

you get to choose
your point of view
you get to choose
to be in a good mood
you get to choose
how you wear
your attitude
i hope you choose
to live all of your days
with a heart full
of love & gratitude

The Roaring 20's:

we are all getting a little older
and time isn't going any slower
before it's too late
this is your reminder
to love every day harder
pray for your heart's desires
speak up for what you believe in
but know actions speak louder
never allow others
to let you feel smaller
but most of all
know there's nothing you can't do
when you recognize
the potential bursting in you

a grateful mind
is a magnet
for a greater life

there is no deadline
there is only your timeline
and though it may not look like
what you might've had in mind
if you allow yourself
to find peace with time
and enjoy every season
before it passes you by
you might just find
how everything falls together
better than you visualized
because this is *your* path
and when you look back
i hope you can say

i made sure i had
the time of my life

it's quite the miracle
wouldn't you say?
to be able to
wake up today
and set eyes
on a brand new day

you see,
the time we get
is not our entitlement
but a delicate gift given
for us to celebrate

own it
enjoy it
make the most out of it
because
there will never be
a collection of moments
quite like them

above all
don't lose sight
of what *is*
right in front of you
there is so much power
in choosing to see
the art in gratitude

welcome
all the wonder
and the mystery
this life brings
curiosity
is a beautiful thing
and mindfulness
will set you free

greet every morning
eager to build
the life of your dreams
know you are capable
of extraordinary things
listen in moments of stillness
find comfort in your own silence
with inner peace comes guidance

choose to conquer

every limit
fear
and doubt

this life is *yours*

your time
is *now*

what if we treated our minutes and hours
like we treat our pennies and dollars
what if we made our days count
instead of counting them down
what if we stopped living for
paper things and metal coins
and valued the delicate time
we spend on this earth
the same way we treasure gold
maybe then would we finally realize
what *every* single day is *worth*

find the delicacy
in what it means
to be *living*
the joy to be found
in simplicity
and even though
we've become immune
to the miracle
of seeing a brand new day
i hope you don't forget
to *never* wish them away
but to look for the best
in every today
before it becomes
a faded memory
named yesterday

celebrate today
look forward to tomorrow
enjoy this moment wholeheartedly
before it becomes a *memory*

everything that
you choose to do
do it with courage

hope courageously
venture courageously
dream courageously

regardless
of tomorrow's mystery
and anticipation
today's moments
deserve the *boldest*
version of you

true joy
is found
in making
the ordinary
feel extraordinary

after this season is over
i don't want to go back to normal

i want to look at my life
with eager eyes
i want to treasure time
more than nickels and dimes
i want to romanticize
the delicate moments
that used to pass me by
i want to fall in love
with every single day
for the rest
of my life

- *quarantine reality check*

you stay in one place for a moment
while you allowed fear to leave you frozen
because you were never sure of the answer
looked for it in everyone else but yourself
and painted a picture in your head
of what the present
should look like instead
but if only you knew
not living for today
could be tomorrow's
greatest regret

The Everyday Reminder:

focus on everything you appreciate
make time for those you love today
listen to what your heart needs to say
give abundant love with endless grace
savor the sweet when it tastes bitter
find peace within the mystery
the *good* in what is yet to be
allow kindness to fill up your heart
know it is never too late to restart

this life is a wonderful gift
this life is *yours* to live

i think often times we forget
that some of the things
we have today
were once a wish
our hearts had made

there is no secret to joy
it's simply choosing
to begin celebrating
where we currently are
and having faith
in where we will be

because today
is another day
He has made
for us to love
enjoy
and praise

how we create
our best tomorrow
starts with today

i hope the day comes
where you finally find
there is nothing
more valuable
than the present's
presence
the gift
of time
and the heart
of life

don't be in such a rush to get there
that you end up missing
the defining moments
leading up to it

celebrate everything
that makes you feel whole
do the little things
that bring you childlike joy
what is it that you love?
make time to do it more
what you surround yourself with
is a powerful choice
and our time is too short
to not create our own version
of a beautiful world

when you wake up
think about

every day
as an opportunity
as a new start

to get to where you want
and be one step closer
to what you'll become

welcome this new day
with an open mind
and a loving heart
today is only the start

we were given memories
to reminisce
but we were gifted
moments like this
to wholeheartedly *live*

there is beauty in the mundane
in finding value within every day
because what might look the same
is delicate in every way
when you rise with the sun
i hope you take a moment
to see the beauty
in getting to live
all over again

Love yourself

when you look in the mirror
you have to live with
the person staring back at you
and my hope is that
you are showing her great love
that you are complimenting her every day
and using the right words to build her up
because there is power in everything you say
so when you look at your reflection
i hope you unapologetically adore
every beautiful imperfection

choosing to love yourself
is the most important
decision
you will make
every
single
day

you look at the world
for acceptance
and satisfaction
only to realize
it can only
be found
within
you

the sooner you choose to believe

everything you need
already lies within

the sooner you allow yourself

to welcome the life
you deserve to live

happiness is practiced
every single day
because you are the only one
capable of making choices
that invite it in

i hope you are choosing

the right people
the right environment
the right thoughts

i hope you are
prioritizing
self-love

i hope you know
you *are*
in control
and start
loving
yourself
to growth

your heart flourished
after enduring the greatest storm
because it was the moment
you realized
it *was* made whole
all on its own

- *life after heartbreak*

every bit of your past
you were so eager
to throw away
and forget
were given to you
as the pieces
you need
to complete
your masterpiece

- *your story is art*

you are a ray of sunshine
don't let gloomy days
tell you otherwise

i used to watch from ashore
and never wanted much more
because i thought i would sink
if i ever allowed myself to swim

i wouldn't allow myself to climb
there was just so much comfort
in staying low
i feared the height
and the thought
of being able to fly

i refused to take charge
of my very own life
until i started to realize
time was only passing me by
i knew i needed to leave
this baggage i collected behind
and pushed myself to take on the climb

you wouldn't believe
the places i was able to see
the things i started to achieve
and the life i began to live—

there is so much out there
waiting for you
don't sit still

as the world around you
continues to move

choose to love yourself
before you give your love
to anyone else

(you can't pour from an empty cup)

you carry yourself
as if you don't belong
as if you are ashamed
of being the strong woman
that i know you *are*
pull your shoulders back
and lift your chin up
from this moment on
i want you to walk
into every single room
with the same grace
confidence
and power
that lives in *you*

you are all too worried
about what people think of you
but have you figured out
what you think of yourself?

in this life you will have
two important choices to make

to live for yourself
or to live for everyone else

self-growth
is genuinely
an act of selflessness
it is to eagerly crave discovery
of a part of you you've never met
and openly welcome the opportunity
to become the best version of you yet
because when we allow ourselves to grow
we are met with the ability
to serve better
favor greater
and give more
than we were able to before

you are the only you
that will ever live
the only you
to ever exist

don't dim
your own worth
when you were made
for so much more

radiate your disposition
write your own story
grow from experiences
work on your dreams
share your joys
move to your rhythm
walk with ambition

regardless of anyone's permission
start living by your *own conditions*

perfect
is quite boring
and if you pay attention
it's your imperfections
that people love most
it's your messiest wildest self
that you have to learn to love
just as well

you look for beauty
externally
yet your own eyes
are most deceiving
if they do not see
how lovely
you
are

i will not dim my own light
for yours to be brighter
i will not hold myself back
for you to move forward
i will not make myself weak
for you to grow stronger
i will not put myself down
for you to stand taller
i will not make myself small
for you to feel comfortable

you were
my thief of joy
made me question
my very own worth
made me despise
other's highs
while i only saw
my greatest lows
had me criticizing my flaws
while you sat back and watched
as i teared myself apart
i looked at others
and i constantly wondered
how can i be
anything but me
i simply couldn't
stop *comparing*
but it wasn't until i chose
to value my own worth
instead of questioning
how happier i'd be
if only i had more

my gold may look different
but it will always be *golden*

i hope you never lose yourself
trying to find someone else
because you
were made
whole
all on your
own

i chose to stop caring
about what people said
because they did not deserve to hold
that kind of power over my head
i chose to stop wondering
about what people thought of me
i was too busy building & living
the life of my *dreams*

true beauty
does not fade
it is strong
bold
and walks with grace
the world can not define
what is one of a kind

true beauty

is resilient
selfless
and brilliant

perhaps
unrecognized
by shallow minds

though,
a masterpiece
painted with *life*

Adversity

don’t let the distance
between where you are
and where you want to be
discourage your heart
and cause you to freeze
it takes grit
perseverance
and endurance
to open doors
that take you places
you’ve *never been*

yesterday's dirt and thunderstorms
are what tomorrow's flowers
need to grow

i've grown to welcome
every *wrong* decision
each one gave me
a little more wisdom

i’ve grown to welcome
every *no* i receive
they've taken me
to every *yes* i need

i don't just welcome failure
i invite it in
with an open heart
and an open mind

because everything that went wrong
has lead me to what was *right*

our greatest fears
stem in what is
unknown
obscure
and untold
but maybe if we grew
curious
fearless
and *fascinated*
by the thrill of not knowing
we would find peace
within the mystery
and begin living

to live in fear
is to not live at all

let go

of this anxious need
to know what happens next
simply keep hope
for all the best
open yourself to the curiosity
of new beginnings
make your peace
with every ending
welcome each coming morning
as a new start and an opportunity
to get to where you want
practice letting go of control
and accepting guidance

take it in
day by day
with courageous hope
and relentless faith

whenever doubt begins to fill your head
own your thoughts and *know* your strength

when the floor seems to be crumbling beneath
take a few minutes in silence to breathe

when you can't find the reason
know there's an ending to every season

trying times do not last
soon they will be your past

and resilient you will become
from everything you've overcome

today i am
thankful for another day
and better than yesterday
still learning from past mistakes
while letting go of any regret
because everything
i've been through
has given me my roots
and made them
stronger than ever
each trial and error
has made me
better and better

sometimes we have to taste the bitter to *savor* the sweet

if you look for contentment
in things you do not control
you'll lose sight
of what every season is worth
and happiness
will come in storms
all at once
then none at all

sometimes the most
inconvenient situations
are there
temporarily
to favor you
enduringly

welcome every season of trial
with patience and understanding
each is there to prepare us
for where we are going

i know you feel unseen
but you have not met
the beautiful days
you have yet to live
this pain you feel today
is not permanent
it's not here to stay
what you feel is temporary
although our hardest seasons
are sometimes necessary
in pushing us to become
anchored and strong
but don't let these times
darken your brilliant light
keep fuming
keep illuminating
keep revealing
your resilience

do not hold regret for the things already done
it stems the roots where you bloomed from
every choice ever made
has brought you to where you stand today

tall
bold
and colorful

with roots strong enough to hold
the force of any coming storm

you are exactly where you should be
nothing worth having comes easy
you are stronger than you can imagine
the best days have yet to happen
adversity comes and goes
but it’s your resilience through it all
that will take you places
you’ve only seen
in your wildest dreams

with every victory
there are

challenges
no's
and setbacks

so when your results
do not look
like your expectations
i hope you remember

the bigger the mountain
the greater the view

don’t get caught up
in your fears
a worried heart
drains your energy
my dear

some doors had to shut in our face
for others to open when we least expected
some things had to fall apart
for better ones to fall into place
sometimes the universe doesn’t give us what we want
so it can give us exactly what we need instead

even on the cloudiest days
the sun never goes away
it sits behind and it rests
but you begin to miss its rays
and once it comes out again
you find overwhelming joy
on a warm sunny day
because you too
have felt the rain

Faith

believing when you don't see it yet
is *faith*
persisting when you want to quit
is *strength*
but jumping without knowing
what lies below your feet
is *courage*

every time you thought you couldn’t
there was this fire inside of you
fighting to make it happen
and even the greatest gale of doubt
was never strong enough to put it out
because what once made you afraid
was conquered with faith
and moved every mountain
that stood in your way

i’ve realized
the realest things
are not those
that can be seen

like the love
we give and receive
and the air that we
continue to breathe
it’s indiscernible
yet without it
we can not live

and you might say
faith is hard to believe
but for me
the realest
most powerful
experiences
were never made
to be seen

your existence
is everything
but a coincidence

i felt God today
it was comfort
it was peace
i heard God today
it was soft
it was sweet
i see God every day
in the land, birds and trees
He's living
with us daily
He's beating
in you & me

what if we turned
every future driven question
that triggers apprehension
into an exciting and hopeful wonder
maybe then we can finally look forward
to this great unwritten adventure of our own

being scared
is not a sign of weakness
but the realization
that what you are about to face
is a powerful reflection
of the great unknown
yet you look at it in the eye
and continue to fight
because the word afraid
can only be weakened with courage
and conquered through strength

when you feel like there is nothing left
place your hand upon your chest
with every beat that you feel
is proof you are *here*
i hope in this you find the strength
to without a grain of doubt believe
your existence is a powerful thing
this life is everything but an accident
it's the most beautiful yet delicate gift
for you to wholeheartedly live
there is no one woven like your fabric
you are pure *magic*

be still in the gift of prayer
look forward without doubt
keep on with faith and courage
move past what you can't control
ask for wisdom in what you can
find peace where you are standing
but most of all *keep on going*
your journey
is one worth knowing

i ask for courage
to overcome change
i ask for strength
to start over again
i ask for wisdom
for the hard decisions
that need to be made
i ask for peace
to fill my head
most of all i ask to live
all of my days
by grace through faith

in a season of most uncertainty
i found myself living in harmony
because i finally learned to let go
of the *illusion* that i was in control
i learned to walk with faith
into the consuming unknown
i learned to love every day harder
because the present moments
are the only ones that matter
i learned to find peace in today
and started believing
in the promise of tomorrow

every mountain you face
is an opportunity
to greet with grace
practice patience
conquer strength
move with faith
and overcome
with perseverance
but no eminence
will ever defeat
your resilience

i can't tell you
how many times i prayed
for some of the things
i have today
but if i can tell you
one thing i learned
along the way
is that faith
is all it takes
for you to keep going
when you feel
like there's no strength left
because even then
you still *believe*
the most beautiful days
have yet to be lived
and every day
you've been given
is nothing less
of an opportunity
and new beginning

it's simple to look
at the circumstances
in this chaotic world
and settle to think
we might be alone

but i'm having trouble
believing simplicity
is what we live in

or that it all aimlessly
collided and came to be
in an unexplainable incident

to believe in yourself
is to believe
you are part of something else
something greater than you and i
more powerful than this life
to believe in you
is to believe in Him too

what if
you are the mountain
and what if
all you need
is a little faith
to get out
of your own way

Keep Going

your future self will thank you
for all the things you do today
to build a life you value
even if it feels so far away
every step you take
is how you create
your own version of fate

it’s a journey
not a race
keep going
at your own pace

don't let your joy

for what is yet to come
get lost in-between
the *what if's*
and c*ould be's*
that you give
permission to exist

instead
begin looking forward
to what comes next
it might show up
so much better
than you could ever expect

be proud of how hard
you're working
to get to
where you
want to be

after all
we are never
a finished piece

you don’t have to know
how it's going to work
no one ever knows
when or where
it’s going to occur

they just keep
immense faith
in their purpose
they believe in *it*
with every ounce
of their being

then

piece by piece
day by day
their perseverance
draws the way
to something
overwhelmingly
magnificent

the rhythm
of our
everyday
routines
has the energy
to bring us closer
to our dreams

i questioned
how do i know?
if i'm pushing myself
enough to grow

but then i thought
about how painfully
uncomfortable
it was for me
to persistently
keep walking
into the unknown
without ever
looking back
at the comfort zone
that used to
freeze my bones

how wonderful it is
that we have the power
to create our own reality
everything we wish for
we have the capability
to persistently work for
and even though
we may not immediately
reap what we sow
every day we push
ourselves to grow
takes us closer to
where we want to go

you are here
to bring existence
to every idea
and every dream
you are here
to make a
beautiful
difference
to detach
from all
the doubt
living in
your head
and overcome
every limit
you created instead

because
what you are
capable of
is resilience
and where
you are going
takes perseverance

you can have all the talent in the world
but how hard are you willing to work?
to get to where you want to go

fear
will leave you frozen
perseverance
will see doors open

if you stopped
letting other's thoughts
influence your own
left the past
where it belonged
pushed whatever limits
you created for yourself
chased your dreams
instead of leaving them on the shelf
if you fully lived for yourself
regardless of anyone else
you would finally know what it's like
to have your own happiness *prioritized*

if you never try
then you'll never know
the things you'll become
the place you'll go

there's some kind of magic
that comes with the courage
to push yourself to keep going
when you just don't know
how you are going to get
to where you want to go

yet you don't lose enthusiasm
and you don't lose hope
because you feel it
deep in your bones
that your time is coming
and it is coming
when you least
expect it to show

the most incredible stories
are not made from milestones
reached with speed
but how every failure
brought you to succeed
keep writing your story
about how you fought
against all odds
to turn those dreams
into your wildest reality

perseverance is all you need
and the resilience to never quit
because you are going to fail
again and again
until you succeed

i hope you never
come to underestimate yourself
enough to let your dreams
collect dust on a shelf
then convince yourself
they were too hard to reach
when you were the one
who left them there
as if it was something
you could never achieve
(we are our own enemy)

there is no promise in waiting
although good timing
needs patience
time is not given
for us to waste it
good things come
when we choose
to do whatever it takes
with what we already have
and persistently
do everything we can
to turn those dreams
into devoted plans

- *good things come to those who go after them*

in your life
you will come face to face
with many mountains
in your way
and you will have
two important decisions to make
to turn around and surrender
or to take on the climb
and let curiosity be the drive
that keeps you going
until you see what lies
on the other side

it's not about finding perfect
it's about finding *progress*
and to progress is to move forward

it doesn't matter how fast or slow
it's not about the pace you go
it doesn't matter if you have to hit pause
it doesn't even matter if you get lost
what matters is that you *do not stop*
that you let your imperfections
create their own directions
to take you to beautiful destinations

whatever you're doing
remember why you started
and *keep going*
if you need to slow down
to find your sound
remember
it doesn't matter the pace
this journey is not a race
forward is forward
before you know it
you'll be standing far beyond
the place you had begun

save the energy
spent dwelling on
how things could be
instead allow your heart
to find peace
where you are currently
you need to believe
in your journey
you are on your way
to the extraordinary

if you’ve failed time after time
this is your reminder
that you *are* doing something right
because those who are too scared to fail
have never dared to try
going after the endless opportunities
that passes them by
every single failure
is a guiding light
paving the way
to your dream life
i hope you’re driven enough
to keep willing to try
time after time
until you get it right

Believe In You

your thoughts
are a powerful
form of energy
a delicate magnet
that attracts reality

so when you close your eyes
i hope you begin
to consciously visualize
your most beautiful
fulfilling
radiant
life

there's a world
of opportunity
waiting for you
to believe in *it*

do not convince yourself
into believing you can’t
there is only trial and error
then there are bones
frozen
at the thought
of failure

if there were no limits
to your capabilities
if there was no such thing
as impossibilities
if you truly fully believed
there's absolutely nothing
you can't achieve

where would you be?

what we think
we can accomplish
is only a fraction
of what we are capable of

- *think bigger*

the hardest part
is moving past the fear of
what if i fail
and start focusing on
what if i learn
what if i give it all i've got
what if i take as many shots
and learn from each loss
what if i need to fail
a multitude of times
to get to where i want
in this life of mine

if you are too afraid
of making a mistake
keep in mind
staying in the
same place
could become
tomorrow's
greatest
regret

your strength
is your power
in overcoming
any impossibility
this world said *it'd* be
because i know
they have not met
your relentless capability

don't be scared to dream

but dream big enough
that it makes you afraid
then be brave enough
to do it anyway

wild opportunities
courageous experiences
infatuating adventures

welcome us
when we grow comfortable
with being uncomfortable
when we believe
in what we can't yet see
and allow ourselves

to
dream
big

success begins
where self-doubt ends

whatever you ask for in life
believe in *it*
believe in its timing
believe its purpose
believe in the journey

most of all
believe in you

by giving gratitude
for all the wonderful things
you have yet to receive

show up as the person
you are striving to be
allows yourself
to go after the extraordinary
you are here
to unapologetically persist
to believe in your abilities
and conquer said impossibilities
within is everything you need
to live out your wildest dreams

i hope you never come to limit yourself
because those don't truly exist
unless you give them permission to
and like time

it's an illusion

of
how
when
and where
you should live your life

so without a limit

allow yourself
to start *living it*

gather the courage
have the audacity
the heedless nerve
to do all the things
that scared you before
our time is far too short
to watch it pass by
and never get to know
our true potential

to doubt yourself
is to also doubt
the creator

who saw void
and made it whole

who saw darkness
and gave it light

who took dust
and created life

take a look above
at all of our stars

every name is called
with absolute love

and their iron
runs in your blood

you are here to do the extraordinary

the most rewarding experiences
will greet you
when you put yourself out there
when you stop caring about what people think
and start bringing purpose to your dreams
when you break free from fear
and give yourself permission
to unapologetically *live*

bloom into the best version of you and remember there's nothing you can't do

we have the ability
to change our life
one choice
one habit
one day
at a time

i think you're capable
of quite possibly anything
yet to you
it's the scariest thought
you could ever admit

waiting for the right moment
might leave you frozen

you will never feel ready
it will never feel right

but nothing
will keep you up at night
more than knowing
you didn't even try

try
even if you don't know what comes next
try
even if you can't see it yet

find your strength
to do whatever it takes
and go after it
because if not now
then *when*?

when you stop believing
the lies doubt tells
you might actually
surprise yourself

all that doubt in your head
is taking up too much space
to let you see
everything you have
the ability to be

be brave enough to dream
have the courage to believe

within you
is everything you need
to create your own reality

with a head full of dreams
picture your life
as the most beautiful being

i think people truly flourish
once they no longer allow
external circumstances
define who they are

there is
so much
abundance
in this universe
everything
you dare
to ask *it* for
you deserve

believe in people
in all of their

dreams
passions
and capabilities

your faith in them
might be the spark
they need
to light this world up

it's when you have gratitude
for what is yet to be yours
that you allow yourself to receive
things you used to wish for
and welcome doors to open
to places you’ve never been before

don't lean
into *their*
fearful doubt
when they
haven't met
your limitless
potential

believe in what you do
believe your heart’s desires
will come true
but most of all
believe in
the power
of *you*

Life is far too delicate to not fall in love with.

I spent my whole life wanting to grow up, and when I finally did, all I wanted was to turn back the time and revive that childhood joy and curiosity that we all started with. That beautiful excitement that used to live in all of us, until it softly faded as we grew older. I found myself wishing my days away, instead of falling in love with what was in front of me, and seeking the beauty in all of my surroundings. You see, once a moment passes, it never comes back, and there is nothing I find to be more delicate than that. In a way, I'm almost fascinated by knowing we have no control over time. To me, it's a reminder that we should do all that we can to not let it ever slip by. It's not something we're entitled to, but an everyday miracle. And it's ironic how they tell us to watch the way we spend our money, even though it always comes it always goes. But I think we should be more concerned about how we spend our time here on earth. When we shift our attention to romanticize where we're at and what we have, it's almost as if everything around us multiples. And I think that's the foundation to building a life of wealth.

Adore everything that makes you who you are. Obstacles are an opportunity for you to overcome. What feels out of your control will only humble you. But your resilience will surprise you. Once you fully believe in the power of you.

Lesley Diana is a poet, writer and creative director from Dallas, Texas. Since the age of five, lyrical art has been something she has loved to create as a form of self-expression. Throughout the years she has collected hundreds of verses, lyrics, and poems without knowing what to do with them. Until she started her journey in writing 'The Power of You'

"The art of connecting with other humans through words and emotions has always been something so magical to me. I want to write the kind of poetry that makes you want to get up and start living your life, one-day-at-a time, instead of watching it pass by right in front of your eyes."

Made in the USA
Las Vegas, NV
12 October 2023